D0854887

Lost in a RAIN FOREST

by Michael Burgan

Consultant: Adam Bauer-Goulden
President, Rainforest Rescue Coalition
Chicago, Illinois

PUBLISHING

New York, New York

Credits

Cover and Title Page, © Dudarev Mikhail/Shutterstock, © Ralph Loesche/Shutterstock, © Steve Collender/Shutterstock, © Videowokart/Shutterstock, and © Aleksey Stemmer/Shutterstock; 4, © Jody Amiet/AFP/Getty Images; 5, © Jody Amiet/AFP/Getty Images; 6, © Nick Gordon/Nature PL; 7, © Reptiles4all/Shutterstock; 8, © Jody Amiet/AFP/Getty Images; 9, © AFP/Getty Images; 12–13, © Sergey Uryadnikov/Shutterstock; 13CR, © DeAgostini Picture Library/Getty Images; 13B, © Tim Martin/Nature PL; 14, © Coleman Rayner; 15, © Coleman Rayner; 16, © BMJ/Shutterstock; 17, © Murray Cooper/Minden Pictures/FLPA; 18C, © Pete Oxford/Nature PL; 18B, © Coleman Rayner; 19, © Coleman Rayner; 20, © Guentermanaus/Shutterstock; 21, © Reuters/Corbis; 22, © Mark Newman/FLPA; 23CR, © Worlds Wildlife Wonders/Shutterstock; 23B, © Frans Lanting/FLPA; 24, © Arco Images GmbH/Alamy; 25, © Frans Lanting/FLPA; 26, © Alex, Segre/Alamy; 27, © Suzi Eszterhas/Minden Pictures/Corbis; 28, © Tomasz Kozal/Shutterstock; 29, © Ben Heys/Shutterstock.

Publisher: Kenn Goin
Editor: Jessica Rudolph
Creative Director: Spencer Brinker
Design: Brown Bear Books Ltd
Photo Research: Brown Bear Books Ltd

Library of Congress Cataloging-in-Publication Data in process at time of publication (2015)
Library of Congress Control Number: 2014012052
ISBN-13: 978-1-62724-291-2

For more information, write to Bearport Publishing Company, Inc., 45 West 21st Street, Suite 3B, New York, New York 10010. Printed in the United States of America.

10 9 8 7 6 5 4 3 2 1

Contents

Hopelessly Lost

In February 2007, Loic (loh-EEK) Pillois and Guilhem (gee-EM) Nayral, both from France, were hiking in a **rain forest** in French Guiana, in South America. As they walked, the men hacked at thick vines with a **machete**. Because it rained so much in the hot forest, the two friends often had to walk through huge puddles.

The rain forest in French Guiana gets about 95 inches (2.4 m) of rain every year. Hawaii, the rainiest state in the United States, gets about 64 inches (1.6 m).

Loic (above) and Guilhem had planned to hike about 78 miles (126 km) through the forest.

Loic and Guilhem were on the last day of an 11-day hike. They had planned to reach the town of Saül that day, but along the way they had gotten lost and were now out of food. Loic and Guilhem did not want to get even more lost. So they decided to stay where they were and set up camp. Would rescuers be able to find them?

When Loic and Guilhem did not arrive in Saül on the last day of their planned hike, French Guiana officials sent rescuers into the forest to find them.

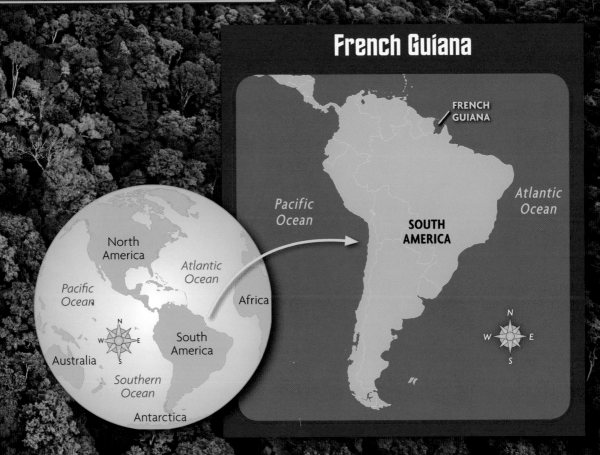

French Guiana

FRENCH GUIANA

Pacific Ocean

Atlantic Ocean

SOUTH AMERICA

North America

Atlantic Ocean

Pacific Ocean

Africa

South America

Australia

Southern Ocean

Antarctica

Food in the Jungle

With no food left, Loic and Guilhem searched the **jungle** for something to eat. They knew that some plants are **poisonous**, so they made a plan. One of them would first take a few bites of a plant. If he didn't get sick, the other would try it, too. Guilhem and Loic also trapped and ate small creatures, such as beetles, frogs, and turtles. They even caught a tarantula! They cooked the giant spider to burn off its hairs, which can **irritate** a person's mouth and throat.

Guilhem and Loic caught a large tarantula similar to this one. This picture shows a tarantula eating a snake.

The two men stayed at their camp for weeks. Occasionally, they would hear helicopters, so Loic started a fire to help rescuers spot them. Unfortunately, the thick forest **canopy** above them shielded the fire's smoke from the pilots' view.

After three weeks, the men gave up hope of ever being rescued. They decided to try to walk to Saül again. They hoped that this time they would be able to find the town.

Loic and Guilhem did not eat animals they knew were harmful, such as poison dart frogs. One kind of dart frog has enough poison in its skin to kill up to ten people!

After a few weeks with no success, the search to find Loic and Guilhem was called off. Officials believed the hikers were dead.

Rescued at Last

During their hike to find Saül, Guilhem caught another tarantula. However, this time he didn't cook the spider long enough to burn off all its hairs. When he ate it, terrible pain shot through his mouth.

Loic was worried. Guilhem was hurt and also extremely weak from not having eaten enough food. He needed medical help. Loic made a tough decision. He would leave Guilhem behind to search for help. Amazingly, two days later, Loic reached Saül!

second from
soon after
ched Saül

Loic made it to Saül after being stranded in the rain forest for almost two months. He immediately contacted rescuers, who quickly found Guilhem and flew him by helicopter to a hospital. Doctors at the hospital said Guilhem would have died soon if he hadn't been rescued.

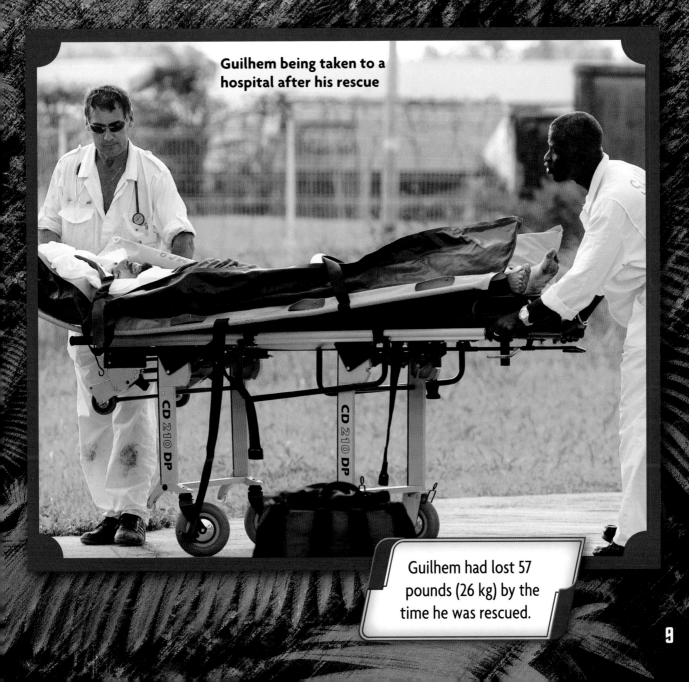

Guilhem being taken to a hospital after his rescue

Guilhem had lost 57 pounds (26 kg) by the time he was rescued.

What Is a Rain Forest?

Most of the world's rain forests, like the one in French Guiana, are located near the **equator**. The weather in this area is usually warm, **humid**, and very rainy. Rain forests get at least 75 inches (1.9 m) of rain every year. As a result, tall trees and other kinds of plants are able to grow there.

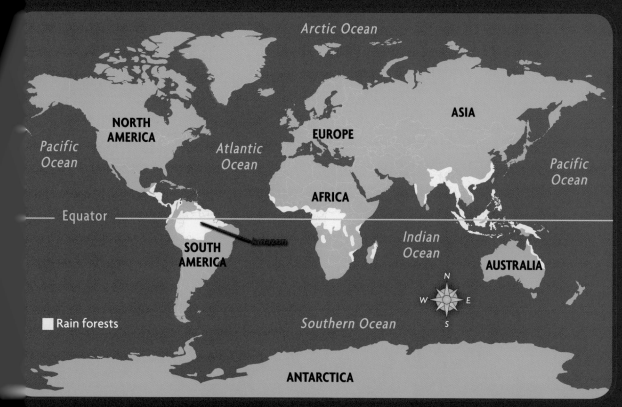

Major Rain Forests of the World

Arctic Ocean

NORTH AMERICA

EUROPE

ASIA

Pacific Ocean

Atlantic Ocean

Pacific Ocean

AFRICA

Equator

Indian Ocean

SOUTH AMERICA

AUSTRALIA

Rain forests

Southern Ocean

ANTARCTICA

Rain forests cover about seven percent of the land on Earth. The world's largest rain forest is the Amazon, in South America.

Rain forests have four layers of **dense** plant life. The **emergent** layer is at the top. Here, the forest's tallest trees poke through the layer beneath—the canopy. In the canopy, treetops grow close together, preventing much sunlight from reaching the lower layers. The **understory** layer contains trees that have not reached their full height. The dark forest floor is the bottom layer. Few plants grow there because little sunlight reaches it.

Layers of a Rain Forest

Emergent Layer— The layer made up of the tops of the tallest trees.

Canopy Layer— The layer containing most of the treetops.

Understory Layer— The layer made up of the tops of young trees.

Forest Floor— Little light comes through the canopy to reach this layer.

Many plants have **adapted** to the rain forest. Some vines grow upward on trees to reach sunlight in the canopy. Short plants have large leaves to catch the little sunlight that reaches the forest floor.

Wildlife in the Forest

Like the plants that grow in the rain forest, many animals have also adapted to living there. Monkeys and apes spend much of their time in the trees. Here they can find fruit to eat and stay safe from **predators** that live on the ground, such as leopards or crocodiles.

Because large areas of the world's rain forests have not been explored by people, scientists are discovering new **species** of animals in the forests every year.

Bonobos are a kind of ape. They live only in the rain forests of central Africa.

Other animals in the rain forest use **camouflage** to survive. For example, the fer-de-lance is a dangerous snake that blends in with leaves and bark. As it hunts on the forest floor, the snake cannot be seen by **prey**. Similarly, the dead leaf butterfly is brown and looks like a dried leaf. Birds and other animals that might want to eat this insect are fooled and leave it alone.

Dead leaf butterflies live in the rain forests of Asia.

Fer-de-lance snakes live in the rain forests of Central America and South America.

Falling From the Sky

The wildlife of the rain forest brought 17-year-old Juliane Koepcke and her family to South America in 1971. On December 24, Juliane and her mother took a plane from Lima to Pucallpa, Peru. Juliane's father was studying wildlife at a nearby jungle **research station**, and she and her mother planned to visit him. However, they never reached the station.

Growing up, Juliane (right) spent lots of time in the rain forest with her parents. Both her mother (left) and father were scientists who studied rain forest wildlife.

During the flight, lightning struck the plane. The aircraft immediately began to break apart. Juliane passed out as she and the other passengers fell 10,000 feet (3,048 m) into the rain forest below. When Juliane awoke on the ground, she was alone. A few pieces of plane **wreckage** were nearby, but she saw no other passengers—not even her mother. Juliane knew she had to find help.

Juliane's parents had taught her how to survive if she ever became lost in the rain forest. This picture shows Juliane as a child walking through the rain forest with her mother.

Juliane had several injuries from the crash. When she woke up in the rain forest, her left eye was swollen, her collarbone was broken, and she had deep cuts on her arms and legs.

A Sound of Hope

Soon after the crash, Juliane saw a stream and remembered something her parents had taught her. People often live near large bodies of water. Juliane decided to follow the stream until it led to a river— and hopefully people.

For several days, Juliane followed the stream, resting on the shore at night. Every day, she got weaker. Her only food was some candy she had found in the plane's wreckage. She was too afraid to eat the jungle plants, knowing they could be poisonous.

A caiman

Juliane eventually decided to swim in the water because it was faster than walking in the dense jungle. As she swam, she passed caimans, which are related to alligators. Luckily, caimans usually do not attack people.

Finally, one day, a loud noise gave Juliane hope—the cry of a hoatzin (waht-SEEN). She knew these rain forest birds build nests near rivers, often close to people. She followed the bird's call and found a large river. Would she also find help nearby?

Hoatzins are also called stinkbirds. The leaves they eat produce a foul smell that covers the birds' bodies.

Signs of People

For days, Juliane swam in the wide river. Because there was no shade from trees, Juliane was not protected from the strong sun. Her skin was burned so badly, it started to bleed. She could barely stand the pain. Even though she was **starving** and weak, she kept going. After ten days of searching for help, she saw something near the shore—a shack! The owners were not inside, but Juliane slept in the shack that night.

Juliane swam in a rain forest river much like this one.

The next day, Juliane heard voices. She stumbled outside and saw three men. In Spanish, she called out, "I'm the girl who was in the . . . crash. My name is Juliane." The men treated her wounds, gave her some food, and took her to a nearby town. Juliane had finally made it out of the rain forest.

In 1998, Juliane visited the site of the plane crash. After almost 30 years, parts of the plane were still there.

Today, Juliane is a scientist. She owns the research station in Peru that her parents worked at.

There were 92 passengers and crew members on Juliane's flight. Juliane was the only survivor of the crash. Her mother's body was found in the rain forest about two weeks after the crash.

People and the Rain Forest

The men who found Juliane Koepcke were **loggers**. Since the 1970s, loggers have cut down millions of acres of rain forest trees around the world. They cut trees to make wood products, such as paper or furniture, or to give farmers more room to grow crops and raise cattle. Unfortunately, this **deforestation** is deadly for rain forest wildlife. When the trees are cut, animals lose their homes and many of them die.

Every minute, loggers cut down an area of rain forest trees that would cover 60 football fields.

Rain forests are also home to small **tribes** of people. Most have little or no contact with people who live outside the forests. Deforestation affects the tribes, too. They lose the land where they live and hunt for food. As a result, the people lose their traditional ways of life.

These Yanomami people live in the rain forests of Venezuela, in South America.

A Vacation Gone Wrong

Like Juliane Koepcke, Brandon and Brandy Wiley became stranded in a rain forest after a plane crash. In 2001, the couple boarded a tiny airplane in Costa Rica, in Central America. The two were on vacation, on their way to take a tour of a rain forest in Corcovado National Park. Altogether, eight people were on the plane.

The rain forest of Corcovado National Park

During the flight, clouds in the sky became thick. Unable to see, the two pilots veered off course and flew the aircraft right into a jungle on a mountain. The pilots and one of the passengers instantly died in the crash. Brandy and Brandon were injured—they were covered in blood from cuts—but somehow survived. As soon as they could get up and walk, the couple searched for other survivors.

A tapir

A red macaw

Some of the wildlife in Corcovado National Park includes jaguars, tapirs, and red macaws.

A Night of Fear

The couple soon found three passengers who were still alive. One man, named Michael, had been thrown 200 feet (61 m) from the crash site and was seriously injured. He had cracked ribs and several other broken bones. Brandy, who was a nurse, used clothes she found in suitcases to wrap his wounds.

The survivors of the crash saw tarantulas crawl by the plane's wreckage and heard the calls of howler monkeys, like these, in the forest.

That night, the temperature fell and it began to rain. The Wileys moved Michael under part of the plane's wreckage to keep him warm and dry. The survivors were hopeful when they heard a helicopter overhead. However, the pilot could not see them through the dense canopy. If the search crew was unable to spot them, was there any chance the passengers would be found?

A jaguar

The survivors worried that the smell of blood from their wounds would **attract** deadly animals, such as jaguars.

Saved!

Early the next morning, the survivors saw lights far in the distance. Could they be flashlights belonging to rescuers? The Wileys gathered up any paper they could find from the wreckage and started a fire with it. Then they shouted into the darkness for help. Soon, they saw a man with a machete cutting his way through the dense forest toward them. They were saved! In no time, more rescuers arrived and took all the survivors to a local hospital.

The rescuers who found the crash survivors used machetes like this one to cut through the dense plant life in the forest.

The Wileys felt lucky. However, it was more than just luck that kept them alive. Like Juliane, Loic, and Guilhem, they survived in the rain forest because they made smart decisions and did not panic—and they were determined to stay alive.

Visitors walk across a rope bridge in a rain forest in Sabah, Malaysia, in Asia.

Every year, many people visit rain forests all over the world. In Sabah, Malaysia, people can walk across rope bridges to see wildlife in the rain forest's canopy.

Rain Forest Survival Tips

If you plan to visit a rain forest, follow these tips to help you survive.

✔ Tell people where you are going and when you expect to be back so they'll know where to look if you get lost.

✔ Wear or pack proper clothing for warm, humid weather. You may have to walk in puddles, so wear waterproof shoes or wrap your shoes in plastic bags. Keep your skin covered to avoid scratches and insect bites.

✔ Pack the necessary gear, such as a first-aid kit, a compass, a map, a knife, and a flashlight. Bring bottled water and canned or dried food. In case you need to drink from a stream, pack tablets that can cleanse water and make it safe to drink.

✔ Bring matches, lighters, or a flint to start a fire in order to cook food, stay warm, scare off predators, or alert people that you are stranded.

✔ If you are in a plane crash, look for items in the wreckage that might be useful. These include food, water, blankets, or a first-aid kit.

Supplies for a trip to a rain forest may include water, flashlights, extra batteries, and knives.

- ✔ If you're lost, follow streams until you reach a larger body of water, where people might be living.
- ✔ Before hiking, look for a long stick. Use it to push aside leaves and branches. It can also help you keep your balance on uneven ground.
- ✔ As you walk, leave a trail so rescuers can find you. You can use torn pieces of bright clothing.
- ✔ If you're on a hill, move downhill to look for fresh water. Drink only from fast-flowing streams.
- ✔ When looking for food in the rain forest, only eat things you know are safe, such as coconuts or citrus fruits.

People who take a trip into a rain forest should use a walking stick and carry the proper gear.

Glossary

adapted (uh-DAP-tid) changed over time to survive in an environment

attract (uh-TRAKT) to draw the interest of a person or animal

camouflage (KAM-uh-flahzh) coloring that makes animals look like their surroundings

canopy (KAN-uh-pee) a thick layer of leaves and branches near the top of a forest

deforestation (*dee*-for-ihst-AY-shun) the process of clearing forests

dense (DENSS) thick

emergent (ih-MUR-jihnt) the top layer of a rain forest, in which the tallest trees rise above the thick canopy

equator (i-KWAY-tur) an imaginary line around the middle of Earth, where it is warm all year round

humid (HYOO-mihd) moist and damp

irritate (IHR-uh-tayt) to cause pain or to make skin turn red

jungle (JUHNG-guhl) a thick forest in a hot place

loggers (LOG-urz) people who cut down trees to sell for wood

machete (muh-SHEH-tee) a large heavy knife often used to cut plants in a forest

poisonous (POI-zuhn-uhss) able to kill or hurt animals or plants

predators (PRED-uh-turz) animals that hunt other animals for food

prey (PRAY) animals that are hunted and eaten by other animals

rain forest (RAYN FOR-ist) a large, warm area of land covered with plants, where lots of rain falls

research station (REE-surch STAY-shuhn) a station built in a remote area where scientists work

species (SPEE-sheez) groups of animals with similar characteristics; members of the same species can have offspring together

starving (STAR-ving) suffering or dying from lack of food

tribes (TRIBEZ) groups made up of many families that share the same language and customs

understory (UHN-dur-stor-ee) the layer of a rain forest above the forest floor; little sunlight reaches the understory

wreckage (REK-ihdj) pieces that remain after something has been badly damaged

Bibliography

Koepcke, Juliane. "Juliane Koepcke: How I Survived a Plane Crash." *BBC News Magazine* (March 23, 2012).

Nayral, Guilhem. "Starving in the Amazon for Seven Weeks." *Outside* (October 25, 2007).

The Nature Conservancy: www.nature.org/ourinitiatives/ urgentissues/rainforests/

Williams, Sally. "Sole Survivor: The Woman Who Fell to Earth." *The Telegraph* (March 22, 2012).

Read More

DeMarin, Layne. *Amazon Adventure (Wonder Readers).* Mankato, MN: Capstone Press (2012).

Littlewood, Peter, and Antonia Littlewood. *Rain Forest Destruction (Mapping Global Issues).* Mankato, MN: Smart Apple Media (2012).

Sandler, Michael. *Rain Forests: Surviving in the Amazon (X-treme Places).* New York: Bearport (2006).

Schomp, Virginia. *24 Hours in a Tropical Rain Forest (A Day in an Ecosystem).* New York: Marshall Cavendish (2013).

Learn More Online

To learn more about surviving in a rain forest, visit
www.bearportpublishing.com/Stranded!

Index

About the Author

Michael Burgan has written more than 250 books for children. He lives in New Mexico, a dry state that is very far from rain forests.